SKATEBOARDING

Jillian Powell

Editorial consultants: Cliff Moon,
Lorraine Petersen and Frances Ridley

nasen
NASEN House, 4/5 Amber Business Village, Amber Close,
Amington, Tamworth, Staffordshire B77 4RP

Rising Stars UK Ltd.
22 Grafton Street, London W1S 4EX
www.risingstars-uk.com

Every effort has been made to trace copyright holders and obtain their permission for use of copyright material. The publisher will gladly receive information enabling them to rectify any error or omission in subsequent editions.
All facts are correct at time of going to press.

Published 2007

Cover design: Button plc
Cover images: Alamy
Text design and typesetting: Andy Wilson
Publisher: Gill Budgell
Project management and editorial: Lesley Densham
Editing: Deborah Kespert
Editorial consultants: Cliff Moon, Lorraine Petersen and Frances Ridley
Illustrations: Patrick Boyer: pages 18–19, 24–25, 30–33
Photos: Alamy: pages 4–5, 8, 9, 10–11, 12, 13, 22–23, 28, 29, 34, 35, 42, 43
Getty Images: pages 6, 7, 20, 35, 36, 38
Version Design Consultants (www.versioncreative.com): pages 40–41
Wig Worland: pages 12, 14, 15, 16, 17, 20, 21, 22, 26, 27, 28, 29, 37, 39, 43

This book should not be used as a guide to the sports shown in it. The publisher accepts no responsibility for any harm which might result from taking part in these sports.

British Library Cataloguing in Publication Data.
A CIP record for this book is available from the British Library.

ISBN: 978-1-84680-186-0

Printed by Craft Print International Limited, Singapore

Contents

Get on board! 4

Sidewalk surfers 6

Skateboard styles 8

Skatewear 10

Basic moves 12

Freestyle skateboarding 14

The Ollie 16

Moonraider – Part one 18

Streetstyle 20

Vert skating 22

Moonraider – Part two 24

Amazing air tricks 26

Parks and venues 28

Moonraider – Part three 30

Moonraider – Part four 32

Skateboard legends 34

Tony Hawk 36

Record-breakers 38

Skateboard competitions 40

More board sports 42

Quiz 44

Glossary of terms 45

More resources 46

Answers 47

Index 48

Get on board!

For some skateboarding is a hobby.
For others it's a street art.

Skateboarding is
a fun way to exercise.

Skateboarders can learn to do amazing tricks on their boards.

Skateboarding is the world's fastest-growing sport.

Sidewalk surfers

Skateboards have been around since the early 1900s. The first skateboards were wooden boards or boxes fixed to rollerskate wheels.

Sidewalk surfer

The sport took off in California in the 1950s. Shops began to sell boards with metal or clay wheels. Riders were called 'sidewalk surfers'. Many skated when the weather was too bad for surfing in the sea.

In the 1970s, skateboards got plastic wheels and **sealed bearings**. This made them faster and easier to control.

Skateboard styles

There are three ways to skateboard.

1

You can skate and do tricks on flat ground. This is called **freestyle** skateboarding.

You can skate in streets
and shopping malls.
You do tricks on steps,
rails and benches.
This is called
streetstyle
skateboarding.

2

You can skate on
ramps and pipes.
You do tricks
on the **lip**.
This is called
vert or ramp
skateboarding.

3

Skatewear

helmet

Make sure your helmet fits well!

elbow pads

knee pads

These have plastic caps to help them slide.

tail

trucks

deck

A rough layer, called **grip tape**, covers the deck to stop your feet from slipping.

nose

Basic moves

It's important to practise basic moves before you try tricks!

Pushing

Stand with one foot on the board. Push off with the other foot. As you pick up speed, lift the other foot onto the board.

Pumping

Stand with both feet on the board. Bend your knees. Move the board by twisting your body.

Slalom or downhill

Ride the board down a slope.

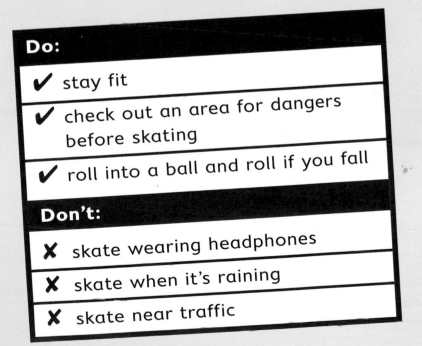

Do:	
✔	stay fit
✔	check out an area for dangers before skating
✔	roll into a ball and roll if you fall

Don't:	
✘	skate wearing headphones
✘	skate when it's raining
✘	skate near traffic

Freestyle skateboarding

Freestyle is the oldest style of skateboarding. It's also called **flatland** skateboarding. It became popular in the 1970s and 80s.

Freestyle skaters do tricks in time to music. Check out these freestyle tricks.

Pogo

The skater uses the board like a pogo stick. One foot grips the bottom **trucks**. The other foot grips the **grip tape**.

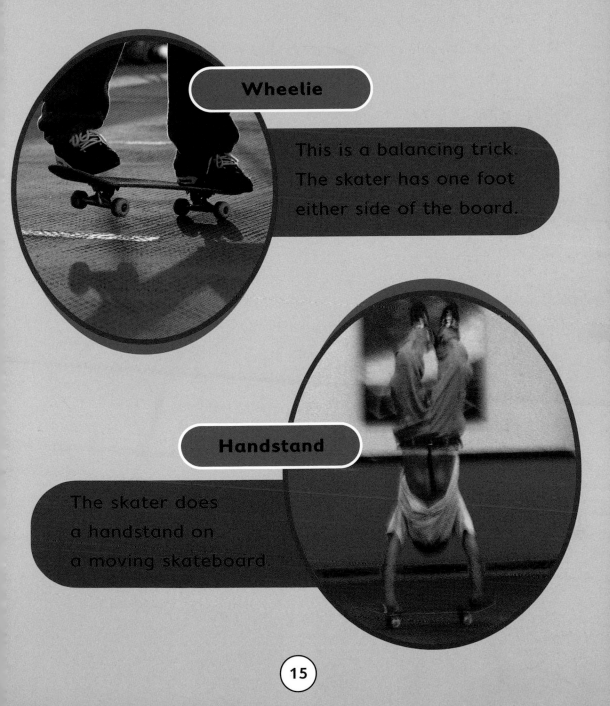

Tic-tac

The skater lifts the front wheels.
The board tilts to one side, then
to the other. As it hits the ground on
either side, it makes a tic-tac sound.

Wheelie

This is a balancing trick.
The skater has one foot
either side of the board.

Handstand

The skater does
a handstand on
a moving skateboard.

The Ollie

The **Ollie** is a type of jump. You have to lift the board without using your hands. The Ollie is the start of many tricks.

1

Push down your back foot to make the tail hit the ground.

2

Slide your front foot forwards to force the board higher.

3 Push down your front foot to raise the rear wheels.

4 Both feet on the board!

5 Bend your knees to protect them when you land.

Skate fact!

The Ollie was invented by Alan 'Ollie' Gelfand in the 1970s.

Moonraider
(Part one)

It was Saturday morning and Joel was working in the skate shop. He loved it there because he got to see all the latest gear.

The shop had a skate team too.
Joel followed them in all the competitions.

He really wanted to skate for them but his boss Andy said he was too young.

"You need more practice, mate!" Andy told him. "Maybe one day."

After work, Joel took his board into the road at home. The road was on a slight hill.

It wasn't exactly **slalom** but …

Clack, clack, clack … he skated downhill.

Mum came out.

"I wish you wouldn't do that here," she said. "That board gives me a headache!"

Continued on page 24

Streetstyle

Streetstyle riders skate in streets and shopping malls. They do tricks on buildings and things around them. Streetstyle became popular in the 1980s.

Kickflip

A kickflip starts like an **Ollie**. The board tail hits the ground. Your front foot kicks the side of your board so it flips over.

Chad Muska is a famous streetstyle skateboarder.

Slides and grinds

Riders use **slides** and **grinds** to slide along handrails, kerbs and benches.

A slide uses the board deck.

A grind uses the trucks.

Vert skating

Vert riders skate on ramps, half pipes and quarter pipes. Vert stands for 'vertical' skating.

Vert skaters do tricks on the **lip**. This trick is called the Rock 'n' Roll.

This mid-air turn is called a Frontside 180.

A skater skates fast before he jumps.

The faster a skater goes, the higher he can jump.

Moonraider
(Part two)

That afternoon, Joel took his board to the library. There were some steps there.

There was even a handrail. He wanted to try a **slide**.

A man came out.

"Sorry, son. You can't do that here. It's too dangerous. You've got a skatepark, haven't you?" he said.

It was true – there was a skatepark with a skatebowl. The trouble was, there were always loads of skaters there.

Joel didn't want to try the bowl when they were watching. He was afraid he might make a fool of himself.

The next week, Joel went to see a film with his mate Danny. It had a great bit of **streetstyle** skating in it.

On the way home, the bus passed the skatepark. It was empty.

The moon was shining on the bowl and Joel had an idea.

Continued on page 30

Amazing air tricks

Air tricks are jumps with tricks done in mid-air. You can do them from ramps and half pipes.

Many air tricks use **grabs**. These are ways of holding the board while you're in the air.

Slob air

The skater turns 'frontside' in the air and reaches round the front of the board. He grabs the deck with his leading hand.

Nose grab

You reach down with your front hand to grab the nose of the board.

Tail grab

You reach down with your back hand to grab the tail of the board.

Airwalk

You jump and make a nose grab as your feet kick apart.

Varial

You reach down with one hand to spin the board underneath your feet.

Parks and venues

Skateparks have ramps, bowls and **moguls**.

In this indoor park, you can ride up the ramp and do a trick, then ride down the other side.

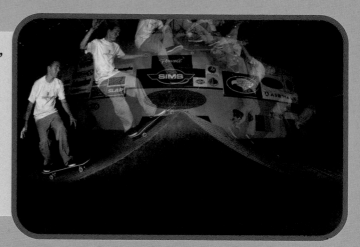

Outdoor skatepark

The 'Livi' in Edinburgh is one of the most famous skateparks in the world.

'Livi' stands for Livingston.

Skateboarding fact!

The first outdoor skateboard park was built in Florida in 1970.

Indoor parks are usually made from wood. They have **vert** ramps, half pipes, bowls and rails.

Skateboarders love cities such as San Francisco and Barcelona.

Moonraider
(Part three)

Beep, beep, beep. Joel's alarm woke him. It was 4 a.m.

He threw on his clothes. It was time to get down to the skatepark.

The moon was still up and the bowl looked a bit eerie.

It reminded him of a moon crater.

Joel picked up his board. He chose one of the smaller ramps.

He held down the board with his back foot. Then he took a deep breath.

The board sprang up under his feet as he pushed down.

He dropped in on the ramp, picking up speed. It felt amazing.

Joel tried again, and again. After a couple of hours, he could drop in at every go.

Continued on the next page

Moonraider
(Part four)

It was the day of the skateboard competition. The skate shop team was there.

They had already won a prize.

"It's the Junior Open next," Andy said. "You should have a go."

Joel carried his board to the **lip** of the ramp. He swept straight down, building up speed. It felt great.

Gliding along the banking, he did a kick turn. The board seemed to know exactly where to go.

He did a perfect **Ollie**, and another. It felt awesome!

Andy was waiting for him.

"That was ... great!" he told Joel.
"You should join our team. You'll need
a name for yourself."

"That's easy," Joel said. "It's *Moonraider*!"

Skateboard legends

Tony Hawk

- Born: 1968,
  San Diego, USA

- Nickname: Birdman

- Most famous trick: 900
  (board spin – two and
  a half rotations)

- Winner: 11 gold medals
  at the X Games

Ali Cairns

- Born: 1975, London, UK

- Motto: 'Fly the fly'

- Most famous tricks:
  McTwists and **lip** tricks

- Winner: Urban games,
  vert series

Andy Macdonald

- Born: 1973, Boston, USA
- Nickname: Mac
- Most famous trick: **Benihana**
- Winner: World Cup Skateboarding competition, eight times

Charles 'Bucky' Lasek

- Born: 1972, Baltimore, USA
- Nickname: Bucky
- Most famous trick: **Heel flip frontside**
- Winner: eight medals at the X Games

Tony Hawk

Tony Hawk is a world-famous skater.
He was born in 1968 in the United States.

He became
the youngest-ever
Pro (professional)
at 14.

Hawk's highlights

- Has entered over 100 Pro contests and won 73.
- Won the X Games vert doubles five times.
- Famous tricks: 540, 900, Madonna grab.
- Has his own skateboard and skatewear brands.
- Makes the best-selling video game 'Pro Skater'.

Hawk has invented more tricks than any other skater.

Madonna grab

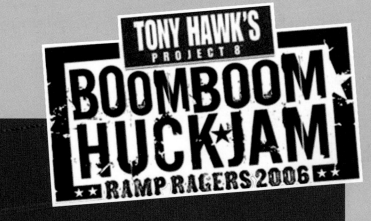

Hawk's 'Boom Boom Huck Jam' tours arenas across the United States. Skateboarders, BMX and Motocross riders perform to live hip-hop and punk bands.

Record-breakers

Top riders are always breaking new records.

Danny Way made skateboarding history on 9th July 2005. He jumped over the Great Wall of China on his skateboard.

Danny also set the world record for the longest distance jumped on a skateboard. He jumped 24 metres at the X Games in 2004.

Highest Ollie

113 centimetres
Danny Wainwright
Long Beach, 2000

Longest Ollie

over 4.5 metres
Danny Wainwright
Paris, 2000

Fastest speed

over 60 mph
Gary Hardwick
Fountain Hills, Arizona, 1998

Most mid-air spins

900 degrees (two and a half rotations)
Tony Hawk
X Games, San Francisco, 1999

Skateboard competitions

Top skateboarders compete in World Cup Skateboarding (WCS) competitions. They win points at each competition. They are marked for their skill and variety of tricks.

There are different competitions through the year.

Mystic Sk8 Cup

This is seen as the best skateboarding competition in Europe. It's held in Prague in the summer. Riders compete in street, **vert** and best trick.

BOARD X

ALEXANDRA PALACE LONDON
WWW.BOARD-X.COM
IN ASSOCIATION WITH

BOARDX SMS
07919 555 437

LONDON BIG AIR

NATIONAL SNOWBOARD EXHIBITION

SNOW GRIND PARK

BMX & SK8 STREET COURSE

MIDI RAMP

XBOX ZONE

Board-X

At this competition, top European riders compete in streetstyle and vert. It's held at the Alexandra Palace, London in November.

X Games

This is the final competition in the WCS year. It's held in August. Riders compete in park, **streetstyle** and vert. They also compete for best trick in each style.

E:0870 902 0444
VANCE:FRI £6.
OKING FEE) ON DOOR:£12
ed trade mark of the Microsoft Corporation

More board sports

Skateboards have inspired new mountain, land and snow sports.

Mountain boards

Mountain boards can be used for **freestyle** or **slalom** skating. The skater's feet are tied to the board.

Freestyle includes ramp jumps, **grinds** and **air tricks**.

Longboards

Longboards can be used for flat or downhill skating. They can cover big distances.

Longboards are bigger than skateboards.

Snowdecks

Snowdecks are
a cross between
a skateboard and
a snowboard.

Snowdecks skate on snow
using a mini snowboard.

Kite landboards

Kite landboards use
a power kite to pull
the rider along.

The power kite fixes onto
the rider's harness.

Quiz

1 What is a grab?

_____

2 What is a mogul?

_____

3 What is a tic-tac?

_____

4 What is an Ollie?

_____

5 How does a skater do a grind?

_____

6 Where is the Livingston skatepark?

_____

7 Where was the first skatepark built?

_____

8 What is Tony Hawk's most famous trick?

_____

9 Who holds the record for the highest Ollie?

_____

10 What is a snow deck?

Glossary of terms

air trick	A trick performed in mid-air.
Benihana	An air trick that uses a tail grab.
flatland	Another word for freestyle.
freestyle	Skating on flat surfaces.
grab	Holding the board during a trick.
grind	A trick where the trucks slide along an obstacle.
grip tape	A rough layer on the skateboard deck that stops your feet from slipping.
Heel flip frontside	A flip trick that uses the heel to flip the board.
lip	The edge of a ramp, pipe or bowl.
moguls	Bumps to skate over in skateparks.
Ollie	A type of jump.
pumping	Moving the board by twisting the body.
sealed bearings	Parts that go either side of the wheels.
slalom	Skating a downhill course around a twisting line of cones.
slide	A trick where the deck slides along an obstacle.
streetstyle	Skating in streets and shopping malls.
trucks	The parts under the deck that turn the wheels.
vert	Vertical or ramp skating.

More resources

Books

Skateboarders Start-Up: A Beginner's Guide to Skateboarding
Doug Werner
Published by Tracks Publishing U.S. 2000 (ISBN: 1884654134)

Livewire Investigates Skateboarding
Kathy Galashan
Published by Hodder Arnold 2000 (ISBN: 0340811277)

Magazines

Sidewalk
A magazine with lots of information on venues, events and gear.

Websites

http://www.exploratorium.edu/skateboarding
The science behind the boards and the tricks.

www.skateparkpages.co.uk
Lists skateparks in the UK with user reviews and video tours.

www.tonyhawk.com
Website of the master with biography, news, links and Q & A.

DVDs

1st step skateboarding – Getting Started
2005 (Cat. No. ASIN B000803PFE)

Tony Hawks' Secret Skate Park Tour
2004 (Cat. No. ASIN B0001LYFW2)

Answers

1 Holding a board during a mid-air jump

2 A small hill or mound in a skatepark

3 Tapping the board on the ground to one side, then the other

4 A type of jump using no hands

5 Slides along an object using the trucks of the board.

6 Edinburgh

7 Florida

8 The 900

9 Danny Wainwright

10 A cross between a skateboard and a snowboard

Index

air trick 26, 42, 45

airwalk 27

Benihana 35, 45

Board X 41

Boom Boom Huck Jam 37

bowl 28, 29

Cairns, Ali 34

competition 35, 40, 41

deck 11

downhill 13, 42

flatland 14, 45

freestyle 8, 14, 15, 42, 45

Frontside 180 22

Gelfand, Alan 17

grab 26, 27, 36, 37, 45

Great Wall of China 38

grind 21, 42, 45

grip tape 11, 45

handstand 15

Hardwick, Gary 39

Hawk, Tony 34, 36, 37, 39

Heel flip frontside 35, 45

kickflip 20

kite landboard 43

Lasek, Bucky 35

lip 9, 22, 45

Livingston skatepark 29

longboard 42

Macdonald, Andy 34

Madonna grab 36, 37

mogul 28, 45

mountain board 42

Muska, Chad 20

Mystic Sk8 Cup 40

Ollie 16, 17, 20, 39, 45

pipe 9, 22, 26, 28, 29

pogo 14

pumping 12, 45

pushing 12

ramp 9, 22, 26, 28, 29

rock 'n' roll 22

sealed bearings 7, 45

sidewalk surfer 6

skatepark 28, 29

slalom 13, 42, 45

slide 21, 45

slob air 26

snowdeck 43

streetstyle 9, 20, 21, 41, 45

tic-tac 15

trick 5, 8, 9, 12, 14, 15, 16, 20, 22, 26, 27, 28, 34, 35, 36, 37, 40, 41, 42

trucks 11, 14, 21, 45

varial 27

vert 9, 22, 23, 29, 34, 36, 40, 41, 45

Wainwright, Danny 39

Way, Danny 38

wheelie 15

wheels 6, 7

X Games 34, 35, 36, 38, 39, 41